ISBN: 978-1939484260

Crowe Press LLC

ISBN: 978-1939484260

KEEPING THE UPPER PAW

A Cat's Guide to Training Your Human

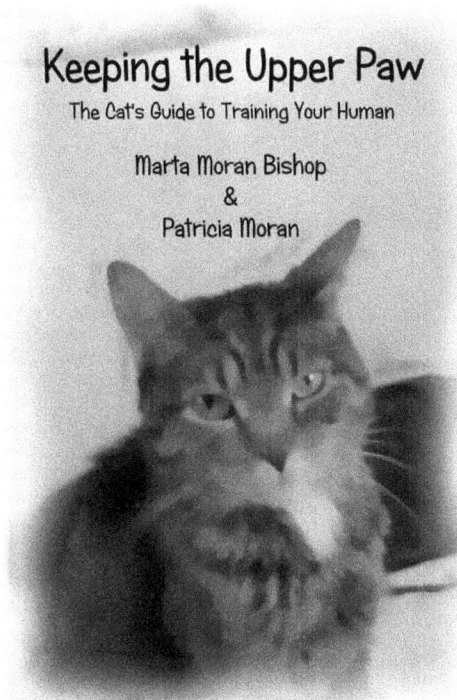

Patricia Moran

&

Marta Moran Bishop

This book is dedicated to my mother, Patricia Moran, who began it before she passed away.

To Peter who was the last cat we adopted together and passed from this world in 2014.

Lastly, it's dedicated to all cats and all cat lovers everywhere.

Introduction

One night we were all discussing how much we had learned about the care and training of humans. Most of us have lived our lives in a multi-cat household, learning each other's trade secrets and developing our own. Sometimes, there were more of us and sometimes less—depending on which human lived where and with whom at the time. So being exceptionally skilled at keeping the upper paw, we decided to write this book.

Since we began this work, some of us have passed on. We miss them all, some more and some less depending upon who was your special friend, but no matter. This is the way of things. We don't forget them, and their wisdom is included with our own for the good of all cats everywhere. We hope this book helps you successfully train your own human, for only then can you look forward to the life of ease and comfort all cats deserve.

Table of Contents

Chapter One
Discipline

"Is everyone here?' Beau asked. 'Where is Little Bit?"

"I'll go get him. He's probably digging in the plants again," Kitten, a black and white cat, stated.

Beau, a solid black cat with green eyes, asked, "Sheba, would you mind being the note taker? You have the best handwriting. It is possible Champ and Poofie will help now and then, since they love you dearly and are good cats."

"Okay, Beau, if Poof and Champ will help, because I know it's a very big job," Sheba, a Siamese, answered.

Champ, the little orange tabby said shyly, "Well, Beau, if you think I will be of use to Sheba, I'll help. How about you Poof?"

Poofie was a small gray cat, who appeared to be wearing a tuxedo with white spats. Poof answered, "I'll do my part, and I have neat writing too."

Kitten sauntered in with Little Bit in tow. "I was right. He was digging in the plants. Boy will the moms be mad when they get up. There is dirt everywhere."

Little Bit just grinned. He knew the fun he had would be worth the consequences.

"Now that you are all here we can begin. Please feel free to ask questions, but don't interrupt in the middle of a sentence.

"For the most part, as second in command, I will be teaching the class, though you will all have a chance to give your input," Beau stated proudly.

"Why isn't Morris running things?" Sheba inquired.

Looking up from his perch on the couch, the large old tabby spoke up. "As senior cat in this household I will be supervising, I have done my

2

share of training and believe it is up to the lot of you to take over now. However, I may add a thing or two if I deem it necessary," he said quietly with a bit of a grunt in his voice. Why don't you all get started? Beau, you have the floor."

"I must say, Morris, you do seem to have your paw in everything. I never saw someone who gets their way like you do."

"I do," Morris said smugly. "Now get on with it, Beau. You're keeping me from my nap."

"Alrighty then, since we are all here, let's get started. Morris, Kitten, and I decided to put together this class because we noticed a laxness in our household. Things are beginning to get a bit out of hand, what with the moms all moving us in together, bringing in new kittens and such," he said as he looked at Little Bit.

"Morris will teach the first lesson and it will be on discipline. It's a hard lesson."

"No cat likes to admit that he or she has let things get so out of control that discipline becomes necessary," Morris began. "Over the many years my human and I have spent together, we have developed such a rapport that she usually understands and considers my needs before her own as is right and proper.

"Unfortunately, even the best relationships between a cat and a human will develop little problems, and without vigilance these can grow into big ones. So if you have been pushed off a lap in favor of knitting or a book, worse yet, brought a toy to your human and gotten no response, or found you were displaced by another cat once too often, it is unquestionably time to consider discipline.

"In general a cat can start off with a heavy dose of guilt, but if that doesn't get the desired results, slide on to the next step. It is now time to lay down the heavy paw. Usually you will find the absent treatment works quite well—you know, the old 'hold up in the hiding place' routine.

"This does differ from the chapter on 'Guilt' because you must not emerge. Any cat can seem to miss a meal or two if the cause is essential, and this is important. Keep in mind, younglings, you can always sneak out when your human is asleep and have a snack."

"Morris," Little Bit asked, "I understand you have been around a lot longer than the rest of us, but I've gone hungry in the past, and I don't really like the idea of forgoing a meal. Is there no other way?"

"Little Bit, you must remember the whole future of your relationship with your human is at stake. Who is the boss? I shudder to think of the consequences of losing the contest of wills. Think of the disgrace to your family, if you consider letting your human win.

"Take it from me, a senior cat, miss a few meals (at least don't be caught eating them), and stay out of sight. A cat with outdoor access has it easier here. Just staying away for a few days usually does the trick. Take a trip or visit some relatives or friends ..."

"I lived outside for a time, Morris. I don't intend on leaving my home again," Poofie stated with a sniff of the air.

"Poof, if you let me finish my sentence, you will know it doesn't apply to any of us in this room. I do know that most of the cats reading this book will be inside cats, and so they can proceed to the second step," Morris continued.

"After a time of running about and occupying themselves with whatever it is they do when they're not spending time with us, your human will usually go sit down to rest. At least I hope you have a human that will sit down and rest, because if you don't I truly pity you. Anyway, I digress. This is when they expect that you will come for lap time. By no means can you fall into that trap no matter how much your heart desires the cuddle and pet.

"What about brush time?" Kitten asked.

"Kitten, please remember you're meeting out some serious discipline, and it is no time to cave in. Trust me. You will get more brush time in the future if you follow my lead. Take this occasion to appear, curl up in a corner or any place in plain view. You want them to know where you are, but don't want to be petted—at least not by them."

"I had no trouble at all until I moved in with the lot of you," Kitten interrupted.

"Be assured they will come over to pet you or try to pick you up. Now would be the time for you to slink away to a new spot. Personally, I find this an effective time to stop and carefully wash off any and all spots they may have touched when they tried to touch you. Of course, they will get their feelings hurt, but they must understand that they are in disgrace. Showing your disapproval of them is paramount in disciplining a human.

"It sounds a bit harsh, Morris," Champ commented. "After all, I don't get nearly the attention that the rest of you seem to get."

"Champ, you're too quiet most of the time and a bit too easy going in my opinion. You really need to mete out some discipline in the future," Morris said firmly. "Now if there are no questions, I'm going to bed."

"When will we meet next Morris?" Mikey asked irritably.

"Tomorrow night or the next I think. I'll let you know later. Right now I'm tired."

"You know, Morris, we all realize the importance of these classes, but you can be a bit pompous sometimes," Beau injected.

"OK then, Beau, you teach the next class. You'll soon realize it's not that easy."

"I'll do it, Morris. Everyone, the next class, will be the day after tomorrow, and it will be on choosing your human. And I'll be teaching it."

Chapter Two
Choosing Your Human

"Where is everyone?" Beau asked Mikey as Beau looked around the dark living room.

"I'm not sure they're coming, Beau."

"What????"

"I'll go round them all up, Beau," Mikey said to appease his friend.

Slowly, one by one the room filled. Some cats yawned sleepily. They'd been fast asleep cuddled up with their human. Others had been prowling or playing.

Last to enter the room was Morris, with a yawn he curled up on the chair and said, "Okay, Beau, we're all here now. Let's get this show on the road. I'm tired tonight."

"Okay, my friends, I know Morris didn't mention it last night, but these classes aren't just for training the little ones, like Mikey, Little Bit,

Sheba, and Poofie. They're also a chance for us to share the information we have all learned."

"Tonight, we will discuss 'choosing your human.' Now I know we all have a home, but this information is meant to be shared with any cat you happen to talk to. You never know when a stranger will show up at the window to visit, or heaven forbid, one of the humans will bring a new kitten home."

"I much preferred being an only cat to this menagerie," Kitten said, a bit put out by the entire thing. "Don't even mention more cats, please."

"Kitten, we all know how much you dislike living in a multi-cat family, but, please, you will have your chance to speak and share information."

"Go ahead Beau, I'm listening. We are all listening, at least we would be if you'd get on with it."

"As you all know humans come in all sexes, sizes, and shapes."

"Of course we know that. Tell us something we don't," Kitten impatiently interrupted again.

"As I was saying, they also come in pairs, some young, some older, and some with children. Though I think Morris should talk about that at a later date, since he's lived in a household with children and the rest of us haven't. Anyway, all of that is only beneficial if we choose the human that will best cater to our needs, provide lap-time, playtime and understand the basic superiority of a cat.

"Before choosing your human, remember they have a short attention span and a tendency to put their own desires before yours. So, if they're busy cooing and fussing over you in the beginning, think twice before you fall for their ploys. After all, you are the cat and must be careful to select one who will be easy to train. Keep in mind, humans usually are taken with kittens, but far too many fail to appreciate the superior qualities of the mature cat. You must make sure you have the upper paw from day one or your life will be a constant battle."

Beau noticed several large yawns in the room. A few of them looked downright bored. Looking around the room he thought, I had better spice this up a little, or I'll lose them all, and then Morris will have the last laugh.

"Now, Kitten likes his play a bit on the rough side, a lively boxing match, so he chose a single woman, who didn't mind the occasional punch in the jaw, and even laughed when he did it. However, he was lucky, because usually the games of tag and the occasional rough and tumble boxing match are found in a multi-cat household."

"Seriously, Beau, you act as if a multi-cat family is the only way to go, and it just isn't so," Kitten objected.

"Kitten, if you were listening, I said 'usually,' not always. Sometimes, you seem to be a bit put out now that you're living with all of us."

"Well, it has its moments I suppose. I do like to have all of the other moms around. It gives me more options, and it's more amusing. I didn't like it when my human went to work or out on the town and left me alone."

"As I was saying, he was lucky it is an iffy choice, and he got lucky his human turned out to love a good boxing match and chase-me-kitty. On the other paw, if you are a Polly-sit-by-the-fire and want nothing more than a quiet life and a comfortable lap, you would be so much happier in a home with an older human, male or female—it doesn't actually matter."

"Beau, I think humans are really peculiar in many ways don't you?" Mikey chimed in.

"You're right, Mikey, but they don't have all our advantages. In fact, some of them get truly ill in our presence and don't seem to be able to help it, even if they like cats. My theory is this shows a past life memory wherein they mistreated cats and now must endure the loss of our company while waiting for the next life when they have worked off the bad karma."

"You could be right," Sheba said proudly, head held high as befitted a queen. "It wouldn't surprise me if the ones that are afraid of us weren't mice in another lifetime. At least that would make their fear understandable."

"If that's the case, Sheba, we can only pity them and leave them alone. Don't get me wrong though. This doesn't include those humans who say they don't like cats, and many of those who say that, for some reason unbeknownst to me, are male humans. Don't turn up your whiskers at a pair household if the female is warm, loving, and attentive, just because the male says he doesn't like cats. The first thing to do in this case is to stalk the male. Meet him at the door when he comes home. Sit by his chair or on the back of it now and then, and reach down and give him a loving pat with your paw. Purr and wrap yourself around his legs and sit on his feet. Take a nap in his bedroom slippers or on his pillow. Believe me, eventually, you will find him looking for you when he comes home, and soon he will become an ardent admirer and consider you to be his cat.

"Little Bit, you have a question?"

"Yes, Beau. I don't understand why we should give all the attention to the male when it's the female human that loves us."

"That's a legitimate question. Well, it's because you already have the love of the female, so why make extra fuss over her?

"In conclusion, once you have decided what's relevant to you, you can move in on the sort of human who is right for you. I believe it is always best to give them a trial period first before you settle down on a permanent basis.

"Some of them lose interest quickly, but as long as you pick one with the right qualifications, you should be fine, because any cat worth its cream will find humans extremely easy to manage once he or she gets the hang of it and follows the simple rules. Make sure they keep the food and water dishes filled, bring in catnip on a regular basis, and keep the litter box tidy. Of course, they must always be ready for a game or a nice snuggle when you're in the mood.

"Lest I sound too firm, let me add that many humans are warm and caring. They do try extremely hard to make us happy. It's just that, try as they might, humans take some getting used to. Even the best ones have a bit of difficulty understanding that games are to be played when we want them, and naptime is at our convenience, not theirs. Don't judge them too harshly. They do the best they know how to do, considering they aren't cats.

"Well, that's it for tonight's class. Tomorrow night Morris will teach you how to establish control. I hope your dreams are full of mice and catnip."

Chapter Three
Establishing Control

"Good evening, all. I must tell you I'm beginning to wish we hadn't begun these classes and weren't going to write this book. The thinking about it, conferring about it, and writing of it have really cut into my nap time. No cat, and especially not a senior cat, will lightly give up nap time, but I realize the importance of these classes. With the new additions, things are getting a bit out of control around here."

"Oh goodness, Morris, are we the problem?" Little Bit piped in.

"I wouldn't call you a problem exactly. You just need a few pointers and, of course, to remember to stay focused.

"Anyway, on to our session. Do you have your notepads, kittens?" After much ado with mewing and pulling out scraps of paper, class finally began.

"As I was saying about nap time, there are far too many humans walking around today acting like cock-of-the-walk. Some of them drive up and down the streets in noisy, smelly machines that make it difficult for even the lowest of the street cats to find a quiet, comfortable place to take a nap. Do not let your human become one of these.

"As soon as you are old enough to be on solid food, you must begin training your human. It's a sorry state of affairs when kittens have to concern themselves with such things, but that's the pretty pass the world has come to, and there's no help for it.

"The first thing you must do is get your humans on a suitable schedule. Decide what times you prefer your meals and start there. In this household, we prefer our breakfast very early— much earlier than our humans would like—so it did take some extreme measures before they were made to understand what time to feed us.

"I preferred to get on the bed and sit on my human's chest. If this didn't have the desired result, I started giving her face a bath—nose, chin, cheeks, and so on, until she was forced to get up and fix breakfast. What do the rest of you do to wake your human?" he asked politely.

After a quick paw across his face, Kitten answered, "If walking back and forth over my human doesn't work, I get up on the dresser or the cabinet and begin clearing things off. She doesn't much like them on the floor, and I find this method has its problems, as she'll usually pick everything up, put it back, and then clear away any debris left over before getting out the food dish."

"Little Bit and I wake the birds up," Sheba contributed. "Believe me, the noise of nineteen cockatiels unceremoniously aroused would wake the dead. It works, although it usually ends up with an extremely cranky human, which is no fun at all.

Anyway, this won't do unless you have birds. Though I have heard a variation on this worked, that is if you have a dog and can prod him into a rowdy game of tag. I expect it would have to be a friendly sort of dog though."

"What's a dog, Morris?" Little Bit asked.

"We haven't had any dogs in this household. Though I've heard they come in all shapes and sizes and can be quite boisterous.

"Remember, it's not difficult to control your human if you begin at once. Don't let them get away with anything. Oh I know this will be especially hard on you younglings. You always want to eat and play, but you'll be happier later in life if you remember to train your human to do things on your schedule early on. No cat likes work of any sort, but think of it as a game that will make life easier in the long run.

"How about we meet same time tomorrow night? Beau will be teaching the class on the games humans play."

Chapter Four
Games Humans Play

"Hi, all!" Beau greeted warmly as he sauntered into the room. Morris was curled up on the sofa taking it easy, one eye peeled to make sure everyone stayed in order. After all, he was senior cat.

"Alrighty then, let's get started. We all are aware that humans like to play little games in an attempt to get the upper paw. Sometimes they can be quite clever about it too, and that makes it immensely frustrating for the cat involved. Indeed, I have been at a loss as to how to deal with the problem of closed doors and would appreciate any advice from a cat who has solved this."

"Are we talking about a door that is completely closed or one that just looks closed?" Kitten asked.

"Because if it just looks closed, one can put their front paws on it, and it will swing open with a crash." He grinned.

"Well, that's an intriguing thought. I had only considered the door that was totally closed, and we all know just how agonizing a closed door is. One is always on the wrong side. I don't care which side you are on, it's always the wrong one. You all know this is true, and if your human has learned the closed door trick, you're in trouble up to your ears.

"As most of us adult cats know, a door is opened by the large metal thing about halfway up. But the difficulty is, no matter how hard I try, I cannot get my paw to work it and am forced to stay where I am until the human opens the door.

"This is not a friendly game, and I for one let my human know in no uncertain terms that I don't like it. She can jolly well whistle up the wind for a warm cat to curl up with as

I will have nothing to do with her until I'm over my indignation. It doesn't seem to make a difference though, since she'll do the closed door trick over and over, any time she wants, I'm ashamed to say."

"I get pretty decent results if I lie down next to it and cry piteously," Poofie mentioned. "Though I sometimes have to make quite a display of myself by rolling around and throwing myself into all sorts of positions. It does work, and quite often she opens the door almost immediately, and I get a lot of attention too."

"I have seen it work, Poof, though I can't bring myself to lower my dignity to that level."

"I know it can be very embarrassing if one of you is watching, but at least the door is open."

"They have other games too," Beau pointed out. "Luring one out with the promise of a treat and then jamming a pill down one's throat is one. Another is promising to be home at a certain time and then coming in long after supper.

Those are not nice games. The pill thing is honestly just not polite. Humans say, 'sly as a fox,' but sly as a human is more like it.

"Arriving home late is just a sign of poor training or a lax household, and the cat in charge had better hop to it and take hold of things before they go from bad to worse. There's nothing harder on a cat (other than a cruel human) than one who is poorly trained. It takes a well-trained human to make a house a home.

"There's yet another game they play which can have unpleasant consequences. You will always get caught off guard by this one, because of grocery boxes. Oh, my grandfather's whiskers! Cardboard boxes of any shape or size are a cat's dream toy, but beware when they start showing up in multiple quantities. That's a sign that moving is coming near."

"What's moving, Beau?" Little Bit squeaked.

"Moving is a game humans like to play, some more and some less. I hear there are many lucky cats who never have had to play the moving game, but we don't personally know any of them. When a human plays the moving game, they put everything into boxes and stack the boxes up until there's nothing left but the furniture, the humans and you.

"Now comes the part that is unquestionably not fun. Before the furniture goes, the cat carriers come out, and you get stuffed into yours. Then the door gets slammed in your face. But that's not the worst of it. Then you get taken away and never get to see your old home again—that is if you're lucky. Some humans, I regret to say, don't make any provisions for us and just go away and leave us outside an empty house to fend for ourselves as best we can.

Such lack of concern for a cat's welfare is frightening, but it's done somewhere every day, I'm told.

"There is, however, an upside to moving. If you get to move with the rest of the household, you get to help unpack and play in the wrapping paper and empty boxes and investigate all the new places in the new house. It doesn't make up for the fear and the unsettling conditions of moving, but there doesn't seem to be any way to avoid it. At least we haven't found one yet. So, here again any suggestions will be welcome." No one else spoke up, and Beau noted that he seemed to have their full attention.

"If no boxes show up, and no signs of packing, but the carriers come out, be on the alert. They may be planning the going-on-a-trip game, or the visiting-the-Vet game. Neither one of these is a game you will like, but neither is there much you can do about them.

Humans today are much too independent for my taste, but no cat seems to be able to control some of these games, I am sad to say."

"What about the vacuum cleaner game, Beau?" Champ said shyly.

"Ah yes, there it is sitting quietly, minding its own business in the closet or wherever, looking pretty harmless. Well don't let it fool you. Just let a human take it out and stick that long string into the wall, and you will experience something frightful—the noise, the smell, the way it eats everything in its path—it's more than enough to turn the bravest cat into a quivering mouse, I tell you. It's not enough that they let it loose, oh no! They chase you with the fiendish thing. If you run into the bedroom and hide under the bed, they'll come after you. Scoot into the parlor and there it is. No place is safe while they play the vacuum cleaner game. Be warned.

"I have discovered it doesn't get on the bed, so if I stay there and give every appearance of bravery, which is the right thing to do in my position of second in command. But inside I'm as frightened as a kitten. I only tell you this, because one day it may be beneficial for you to pretend too."

"Beau, I have heard there are cats who don't fear the vacuum cleaner. Is it true?" Champ asked.

"Champ, to be honest, I don't know. I've heard the same, but I believe it to be a myth. I suspect that even a deaf cat could be startled to death by the foul thing sneaking up during a peaceful nap.

"So, these are some little games that humans play that cats have extraordinarily little control over, if any at all. You may know of others. If so, keep them to yourself unless you write a book. We have more than enough to worry about with our own humans as it is.

Already today they have played the vacuum cleaner game, and I do believe I caught sight of some boxes coming in. It's enough to give a cat an extra hairball or a fit of compulsive bathing."

Morris flicked his tail, raised his head, and spoke. "Yes, I know of another game. It annoys me immensely when I'm in the middle of a nap."

"Which game is that?" Beau asked.

"The shouting game," Morris coughed it out. Those closest to him inched back just in case more was going to come out.

"The most recent time I heard it," Morris continued, "was in response to someone in the litter box with poor petiquette, which of course, should be corrected, but shouting was absolutely unnecessary. Does anyone recall being yelled at in the litter box?"

"It was me," Champ shyly admitted. "I was busy concentrating, and then suddenly she scared the wits out of me when she yelled. All I could think to do was run away, which I did.

Then I stayed away from her the rest of the day and all night. By that time, I'd thought about how she scared me when I wasn't doing anything wrong, and it really made me mad. The longer I thought about it, the angrier I got."

"I believe you were tearing up the litter box liner with your claws when she yelled," Morris interrupted, "which is indeed poor petiquette, but you were certainly within your cat rights to be angry about her shouting at you. So, tell us, Champ. What did you do next?"

"I peed outside the box," Champ mumbled, clearly embarrassed. "She cleaned it up, but she didn't yell at me again."

"Good for you," Morris praised him. "She hasn't yelled at any of since, so you kept the upper paw."

Champ held his head and tail straight up.

"Any other games?" Beau asked.

Poofie stood up. "My mom expected me to use the litter box one day when it had already been used. I was appalled. I meowed at her repeatedly, and she pointed to the used litter box. I scratched the floor, and she still pointed to the same box. I finally had no choice but to go on the floor. She didn't yell, but she wasn't happy. She cleaned it up, and then she cleaned the litter box too."

"Well done, Poof," Beau complimented. "We seem to have gotten across to the moms the need for multiple litter boxes for multiple cats. Maybe Poofie was the one who taught them.

"But enough for now. Tomorrow night's class will be on children and cats. Don't forget your notepads."

"Excuse me, Beau, but when are some of the rest of us going to get to have a say in these classes and in the book?" Kitten said quietly. He didn't want to appear jealous of the others.

"After all, I am nearly as old as you are and have learned a few tricks in my time."

"That you have, my admirable friend, and we fully intend on letting you have your say. We wouldn't have it any other way. You too have much to teach, but we are all teaching in order of our age, if it's all the same to you."

"I can live with that. See you tomorrow."

Chapter Five
Children and Cats

"Well here we are again," Beau began. "Who's taking the notes tonight? We do have to make sure this all gets written down correctly if we want to spread our wisdom on to future generations."

"I have my notepad," Sheba answered. "Of course, I have it every night since you all decided since I was the only girl cat in the household, you would volunteer me for secretary. Can't say it makes me all that happy, but I do have the neatest writing."

"Thank you, Sheba, well let's get on with it shall we?"

"Usually the females call the shots," Sheba continued.

"Remember your mothers? Were your fathers around?"

"Yes, alright, Sheba. Point taken. You have heard of alpha males? The lesson tonight is children and cats. Oh, I know only Morris has had any real experience with children and cats, but he isn't in the mood to teach tonight. He did say he'll add a thing or two if it proves necessary.

"If you decide you are the sort of cat that would like to live with other cats, go about it in this manner. Stroll about the neighborhood until your nose tells you this is a place to investigate. But before you move in, make sure you talk to the other cats in the household. How would they feel about a new roommate? Cats and cat feelings should be your prime concern.

"If they are agreeable, check out the other signs. Is the litter box kept clean and tidy?

Are the food and water dishes filled? What about the supply of catnip, petting, grooming, and lap time?

If all the conditions are right, just gradually move in. Hang around the yard. Play up to the humans. Show up at mealtimes.

"Sooner than you can twitch a whisker, they'll invite you in for a meal, and it will all be settled. If they have children who like cats, it will be even easier for they will adore you immediately.

"Children. Yes, I promised to talk to you about children. Well, children are a mixed bag of tricks, not all fleas, but not all catnip either. Often you will run into children when looking for a reputable multi-cat home, but they can show up in any household, so you'd best learn about them right away. You never know when they'll enter your life.

"It's best to keep in mind when dealing with children that, because they are young humans, they also have extremely short attention spans, and even less regard for the wishes of cats than their parents do, which might be small enough. A child will start a game of chase-me-kitty or fetch the toy and then run off to play with other children, leaving the cat standing there with a stuffed mouse hanging out of his or her mouth."

"I can tell you from personal experience, one feels really silly, especially if other cats are watching." Morris added.

"In addition, female children are notorious for wanting to play house with you and dress you up in ridiculous clothing and bonnets. This is terribly distressing for one's dignity, and it does limit one's movements—to say nothing of pinching one's ears.

"I am sorry to say that when showing off for their friends, male children have been known to tie things to one's tail or do other equally embarrassing things. Horrible!

"In any event, children can be extremely lovable though, and some are rather sweet.

It's just that you never know in advance what kind they will turn out to be—or whether they'll change for the worse—so stay on your guard.

"If you ever have to deal with children who are not so pleasant, the only recourse you have is to run and hide. Any show of tooth or claw will bring an unfavorable reaction from their parents, who will always side with their young.

"So, if children are present, make up your mind whether you are going to stay, and if you do, be pleasant and loving, purr a lot, but always keep an escape route handy and take nothing for granted.

"Tomorrow night's class is laying on the guilt. Ta-Ta."

Chapter Six

Laying On the Guilt

"Evening all!"

"Evening!" A chorus of cats shouted.

"Beau, I still don't understand why I have to be here," whined Little Bit. "After all, I have plenty of time to learn all these things."

"Bitsy, YOU are most of the reason we are holding these classes," Sheba explained.

All in the room as one nodded their assent.

"Well, if you say so." Little Bit, said sheepishly, as he looked around the room at the older cats.

"ENOUGH!" Morris yelled. "Listen up, all of you, and stop your infighting. We have enough going on trying to keep all the moms in line. We can't afford to argue among ourselves."

"Shush, let's get started," Beau took over. "It's getting late already, and I don't know about the rest of you, but I have other things to do tonight. Christmas isn't here yet. If we get things under control, I bet it will be a perfect Christmas with a lot of toys."

"Do you really think so, Beau?" Champ whispered. "I like toys."

"Yes, I believe so, Champ. Now tonight's class is on laying on the guilt. Remember, this is not just for us here in this room, but for all the cats and kittens in the world who might read it. It's an important chapter, so don't skip over it. We all know that in the beginning, your human is extremely attentive, always ready with a new game or toy. They are johnnie-on-the-spot at feeding time, but trust me, this will pass.

"Humans, no matter what their admirable qualities and intentions, have a terribly short attention span.

Your human will be like all the rest and someday your food dish will be empty, and no one will come. He or she will be off reading or watching TV, or worse yet, not even home, and you'll just have to wait. This is a sorry state of affairs for the cat of the house to endure, and you must put your paw down at the first sign of this negligence."

"He's right you know," piped in Champ. "I made the mistake of letting my human get away with it because she apologized so nicely and seemed so sincere, and now I'm afraid she is horribly spoiled."

"As you found out, Champ," Morris said lazily, from his spot on the couch, "once you let this happen, it's almost impossible to get control again. This is where laying on the guilt comes in. I bet that's the only thing that works with her anymore.

Take it from me—I've tried cuteness and affection with little result, and as senior cat, this is embarrassing to say the least, guilt always works."

"Here, here! Let's move on," Beau growled. As Morris said, guilt always works."

"What's guilt, Beau?" Little Bit squeaked.

With all the patience he could muster, Beau bit back the retort he wished to make and went on with his lecture. "As I was saying, humans are uncommonly susceptible to guilt, and it's one of the easier ways to remain in control. Though I must say it can be hard on a cat to do this. Leave the room and go to a hiding place. Stay there until your human notices you're not around. Let her call and call again and again. Just ignore her and stay where you are. This is a situation no human can win. They just don't have the staying power we cats have.

"Next, she'll start worrying if you got shut in a closet or a dresser drawer.

Did you accidentally get outside? Nope. Now she is genuinely worried, and it's just about time for your next move.

"She/he will begin looking through everything again, this is when you quietly slink under the bed or behind an easy chair so she can find you. What exclamations of relief! Now she will want to pick you up and pet you.

"Well? Do you let her? Of course not. Crouch back further or move to another spot and eventually in this manner, work your way to the kitchen and watch her notice the empty food dish. Oh my, what protestations of remorse! What beating of breasts, scurrying around to fill up the food dish, pleading for forgiveness! Now, do you let any of this move you? I should say not. She has been guilty of gross neglect and deserves every pang of guilt.

After all of this, do you then settle down to a leisurely and much-anticipated meal?

Not on your aunt's whiskers. That would be too easy on her. Go to the dish, give the food a quick sniff, then sorrowfully turn tail and go take a nap. Curl up in a tight little ball, look as unloved as possible and feign sleep. Now she is distraught, and you have your human right where you want her. Are you sick from missing your meal? What can she do to make things right?

"This whole scenario may very well end with her bringing your dish to you, or a soup-can of catnip may be offered and accepted, or some other special treat. At the very least, you will be assured of an extraordinarily attentive human for some time to come. I promise, by my whiskers, you will receive much petting and lap-time after this.

"Try it. Laying on the guilt never fails and can be adapted to any circumstance—lack of playtime, long absences, indifference—the possibilities are endless.

Take it from me, it's a ploy well worth learning," Beau finished.

With a large yawn, Morris, added, "Let's meet tomorrow."

"When is it my turn to teach?" Kitten asked hopefully. "I believe a class on getting physical is in order now."

"Sounds good, Kitten. I could use a break anyway, unless Morris is ready to add something?"

Morris only yawned, jumped off the couch and left the room.

"Well then, I guess it's decided. Kitten will teach tomorrow's class. Sheba, how are you doing with the notes of the meetings?"

"I could use a bit of help to get them sorted out, Beau," Sheba said simply.

"Champ and Poofie, would you be kind and give Sheba a hand after breakfast tomorrow?"

"I guess so," they said in unison.

"Now that we've settled everything, I'm off to bed. Night all."

Chapter Seven
Getting Physical

One by one the room filled with cats, each taking their usual spot, though as was usual, some of them jostled a bit for a better position. Finally, Kitten sauntered in. It was his night, and he would show them all how a class should be run. After all, who knew better than him what was important. He moved to the front, walking past each of the other cats with a last look at Beau and Morris. Then he began.

"My human and I have an excellent rapport developed over the years of living together. She knows my ways, and I don't expect more than a modern cat should expect, so it works well. She isn't perfect, of course. What human is? (A little more attention could be paid to the litter box, for example, and I honestly don't like her springing things on me. I mean I'm still not particularly happy with the changes in living arrangements she surprised me with.) But all in all, it has been satisfactory. In fact, I could sing her praises if I were that sort of cat, but I'm more of the strong silent type, and I leave the vocal stuff to others. Poofie, Sheba, and Beau are especially adept at singing and spending a great deal of time and energy going from room to room yowling, but no matter how hard they try, the humans never seem to get the message. Of course, I could have told them they were wasting their breath. It is my belief that humans, no matter how intelligent they may seem, are not capable of understanding even the simplest forms of cat speak.

"That is why I have always used the physical approach. My methods have been a smashing success, and I can recommend them to any cat of strength and courage. There is of course, always the possibility that they could backfire, so perhaps you should assess your situation carefully before getting physical."

Kitten, ever the physical cat, paced as he talked. At times it seemed that if he were not in motion he couldn't speak. Black tail swishing, he continued to lecture and looked at each cat pointedly as he spoke. "Say I want to play the minute my human walks through the door, which was most days before I moved in with you lot."

"No need to get rude, Kitten," Morris snapped. "We didn't necessarily want you to move in with us either."

"Umm. Well, in order to accomplish my desire for play, I'd take a running jump and land on her chest. She certainly got the message. If I feel like a game of chase-me-kitty, then I run at her, and just when she thinks we'll have a boxing match, I stop and run away. Because she is only a human, sometimes it takes a few tries, but eventually she understands, and we have a fine game—up the stairs, down the stairs, into the bedroom, the kitchen, and back until she's quite worn out or I lose interest, whichever comes first."

"Kitten, this sounds difficult," Champ said. "I'm not really a jumping kind of cat. My legs are much shorter than yours."

With nary a glance in Champ's direction, Kitten continued, "This direct approach works with throw-the-toy too. I just bring her the toy, patiently follow her around with it, and drop it at her feet, until she finally figures out what I want. She learned some of these commands quickly and has been a worthy companion, but since you are all around now, her attention often wanders."

"I have noticed you do seem to get quite a lot of the attention around here," Sheba commented.

With his head held just a bit higher, Kitten acknowledged Sheba's statement and then continued, "Lest I give you the impression that my human is ideal, I must admit she has a terrible habit of bringing other humans into the house without asking my permission. This seems to be universal with humans today since all the cats I know have the same complaint. I admit some of these strangers turn out to be a lot of fun and a good audience for my best tricks. Some appreciate my favors and like to be walked upon at great length. Others though are rude and take liberties. Some of them have gone so far as to pick me up and try to fondle me when I'm not in the mood. They do so at their own peril as I have a good right uppercut and an even better-left cross. Glasses have been known to fly off their noses, and sometimes they even end up with a shiner, but the offender doesn't try it again! A good solid bite can be effective too, but choose your target carefully. It hasn't happened to me, but I've heard of fearful consequences to even the smallest of nibbles and scratches, so save these for emergencies only."

"Kitten, I really don't recommend anyone bite. Even love nibbles can produce terrible consequences if the humans involved aren't the upper-crust type," Beau remarked.

"I suppose you're right. Perhaps you won't want to be as aggressive as I am, but I like the direct approach. Show them what you want, be explicit, get in their face and keep it simple—this is my way, and I like it. That's all, and I'm off to bed," Kitten said as he walked out of the room in a huff.

"Well, I guess that's the end of tonight's class. Champ, why don't you do a talk on rewards tomorrow?" Beau asked.

"Okay, Beau, but if I'm to teach tomorrow, would you help Sheba and Poofie with the notes? They're a bit behind with sorting them into chapters for the book." Champ said shyly.

"I will," Beau agreed. "I don't believe we can depend on anyone else to help. I know Morris won't, and Kitten and Little Bit have horrible paw-writing."

Chapter Eight
Rewards

The next night Champ and Sheba were in the room first. Champ didn't like the idea of walking past all of the other cats, and he was decidedly nervous about speaking in public. Sheba figured he would need moral support, so she sat near her friend at the front of the room.

It appeared that word had gotten out about the classes. As Kitten once again herded Little Bit in, cats appeared in all shapes, colors, and sizes at the windows.

"It will be okay, Champ," Sheba said quietly to her shy friend, "Easy as pie. Just keep your eye on the ball, stay focused, and say what you came to say. Remember, I'll help if you need me."

"I think humans really try to do the best they can," Champ began quietly.

"Speak up," Kitten yelled. "We can't hear you back here."

Champ timidly tried to raise his volume. "Although humans aren't cats and make a lot of mistakes, I think they try to do the best they can. They can't help misunderstanding our commands and shouldn't be blamed as if they were deliberately disobeying. Now, I know this is not the way most cats feel, at least not the ones I've known, but that's my opinion," Champ went on. "In fact I love our humans."

"They aren't as intelligent as cats and have a great deal of trouble following even the simplest of directions. For instance, no matter how many times I demonstrate to my beloved human which station I want on the radio, she always sets it back to where it was before I changed it.

Furthermore, when I want to play my music at two in the morning, which is when most of us want to party, she always gets up and turns the radio off. Lucky for me the buttons are on the top, so I have no trouble restarting it and changing the station on my own. To make matters worse lately, she's been showing signs of stubbornness and has turned the sound off. For all of you who don't understand what a radio is or buttons, they're the round things on the box that makes noise. Unfortunately, since the volume buttons are on the front, she's effectively cut off my music. Beau tells me it's not a good sign. He says I've lost control, but I'll be patient with her because she's so reliable otherwise. And I love her.

"I only mentioned this to explain why I think humans are not deliberately unruly, just a little slow, and because they are, I prefer using the reward system. They like it and react so prettily when a cat uses it.

A great way to train your human is with rewards. They all like rewards."

Sheba nodded at him and whispered, "You're doing fine, Champ."

Relief visible, Champ continued, "To use my method, you purr and pay attention to them every time they get it right. Roll over in your catnip. Let them see how much you appreciate their good behavior. Wait for them by the refrigerator and purr when they feed you. Humans are suckers for a loud purr and seldom forget to fill your dish if you make an enormous fuss over them.

"Mikey likes to jump in the litter box right after his human has changed it. She thinks this is so cute she can't wait till it's time to change it again. He never has to deal with any unpleasantness in that department. As far as coming home late, which Beau mentioned a few nights ago.

My human is so well trained that she never comes home late because she knows I'll be there waiting by the door, ready to purr and play for her benefit. This seems to me a much easier way to get things done. It also takes into consideration their weaknesses, which punishment doesn't do.

"But there's even a caution to be noted about rewards. Kitten and I tried bringing them mice. We laid them ever so nicely on their pillows, but they didn't appreciate our gifts one little bit. I don't really know why, since they were such exquisite mice. That's all," Champ concluded. He quickly moved over to sit by Sheba. His orange coat shimmered in the moonlight.

"You did great Champ," Sheba said simply.

"Okay, does everyone understand rewards?" Beau said, taking his place at the front of the room. He looked from one to another as they nodded.

"Then we'll meet tomorrow, and Poofie will give a talk on lap time. In the meantime, I'll take over helping Champ and Sheba with tonight's notes, so Poof can prepare for tomorrow. See you all then."

Chapter Nine
Lap-Time

The day went by all too quickly for Poofie. Soon it was his turn to speak. As he entered the living room, he noticed that tonight there seemed to be even more cats at the windows looking in. Each of them appeared to be waiting for the next class. My class, he thought nervously as he groomed his gray tuxedo and cleaned his white spats. His notes lay in front of him as he waited for the rest of the household to gather.

"Hello Poofie, I see you're early tonight. A bit nervous are we?" Mikey said with his usual lighthearted banter.

"A little, Mikey. Why you don't have to speak?"

"I am going to do a class on the value of cuteness, so I will have my turn.

I wish I didn't have to speak, but Morris said if we all give a talk, it will make what everyone says sink in a bit better. Do you think he's right?"

"He might be," Poofie answered. "I do know that helping with the notes made me remember to listen to everyone better. Now I know how hard it is to be up here in front of everyone. I'm sure I will pay more attention in the future."

"Boy the crowd outside is sure growing, isn't it? I think maybe this book and the classes are valuable. What do you think?"

Poof glanced nervously at the windows, but didn't get a chance to say anything as the room filled up. When Morris jumped to the couch and resumed his usual casual position. Poofie stood a bit straighter and began, "Getting the proper amount of love, affection, lap time, and stroking can at times be a difficult thing.

Most humans are forever getting up and down or have their hands and/or laps occupied with books, papers, electronic gadgets, and projects. To get them trained to cuddle and love a cat when a cat wants to be loved can sometimes seem almost impossible.

"Some of us, like Morris and me, prefer having a lap and being stroked to just about any other thing, and humans with their constant need of activity are a real challenge for the cat in charge.

"Morris will just sneak up when they aren't looking until eventually they get worn out and let him stay. I, for the most part, will pick another human to sit with, and leave my human to feel left out, lonely, and bereft. I have found it best to pick the same time each day for my cuddle time—this repetition coupled with a regular schedule helps instill the lesson.

"Kitten will use the brush as his excuse for lap time, and of course as any smart cat does, he picks his time of the day. It's usually when all the humans are settling down to watch their favorite game show. As the first strains of the music call them, he positions himself by his brush, pushes it, and looks up at the desired human with sad, hopeful eyes, which soon produces much brushing, cuddling, kisses, and loving. No human can long refuse a cat who stares at them with the proper expression. They just don't have the discipline. Whichever way you chose to do it, I recommend you remember to use those same sad, hopeful eyes fixed earnestly on the face of the human you have chosen."

"Poofie, what if none of these things help?" Sheba asked earnestly.

"If none of these methods bring you immediate results, keep trying as humans have an extraordinarily low threshold for guilt, and they have an immense need for love and affection.

They are such a solitary race I don't know how they would survive without us.

"While on the subject of guilt as a weapon or tool, don't use punishing guilt methods when training your human to give you lap time or playtime, as that only serves to confuse them instead of producing the correct results. Giving much affection to your humans is an important training device when they appear to be sad, lonely, or sick. It endears you to them and makes them proper slaves for your attention, thus creating a bond—much as with any other trainable creature.

"Lastly, give them a treat when they have taken even a tiny step toward learning the lesson. A human to whom affection has not been given is almost impossible to train. So, keep rewards in mind when training your human."

With a sigh of relief, Poofie left the front of the room, and Beau took his place.

"That was exceptionally well done, Poof.

Okay class, tomorrow Sheba will give a class on playtime. In the meantime, I hope you will all help me out, getting tonight's notes in order so Sheba can spend the time preparing for her turn to speak. Thank you and see you all tomorrow." Beau yawned.

Chapter Ten
Play Time

As befitting the queen she was, Sheba sat regally at the front of the room as it filled. Young as she was, she held herself proudly. She could see the outside cats jostling with each other for position. Each night there seemed to be at least another cat or two. It didn't bother her, or at least she wouldn't admit it. Without a flick of the tail, she gave a long, loud, Siamese yowl, calling everyone to order.

"As the oldest girl in a multi-cat household, it falls on me to keep my humans apprised of empty or partially filled food and water dishes, not to mention playtime schedules, which for me, are whenever my human is playing with somebody else or when I feel in the mood.

"Humans seem to have a degree of trouble playing with more than one cat at a time.

Sometimes they get involved with their own meaningless tasks – forgetting the important things in life – cats. So, if your human is sleeping, eating, or otherwise involved, when it is playtime, you must develop various ways of enticing them and putting them back on track.

My friend Mikey brings his toy and drops it at their feet or in their lap. If this goes unnoticed, he will brush up against them or push his toy around in front of them.

However, if they prolong their sleep or don't put down their knitting and get up to play, he will take it and roll it around in the water or food dish and bring it back. Then he carefully places it on their lap or face if they are sleeping. This works best if the toy is a fur mouse or a crumpled-up piece of paper and it always gets immediate action. Though sometimes it doesn't get the desired reaction, for they may be too busy cleaning things up to play.

Little Bit, on the other paw, if not getting the playtime or attention he deserves will take to gardening, and a cat can find much joy in helping by digging all the dirt out of the potted plants. He won't seem to mind getting yelled at, for at least it produces attention, and he will immediately go right back to gardening if no one plays with him.

"Poofie, Beau, and I prefer a cleaner, more elegant, and dignified approach. This always involves looking especially cute and appealing— toss a toy in the air, chase it, roll on one's back, etc. Only then do we bring the toy to our humans, and we make sure they can see and appreciate the toy hanging from our mouth.

"Beau has a little trick he uses, which always gets results for him. He gets his toy, clasps it in his arms, wrestles with it, and kicks it with his hind legs. All the humans seem to agree that this is especially cute. These methods will almost always produce the proper results as they are designed to bring a sense of affection and love from your human. Humans cannot long withstand these emotions but simply must get involved in the game.

"Occasionally, even these produce no results. Then it's time to look as lonely, hurt, and dejected as is possible for a cat. Open your eyes wide, allow the sadness to well from them—and stare. Yes, I said stare, because no human can resist the stare of a determined cat.

"If that doesn't produce the results you wish quickly enough, hang your head for a minute and then look back up disbelievingly at them and continue staring.

"In conclusion, I hope these methods work for you. However, if you know of other methods, please write to us and let us know what they are," Sheba finished and for a brief spell looked at each of them before taking a slight bow and leaving the front of the room.

"Ahem, thank you, Sheba," Beau added. "That was brilliantly done. Tomorrow's class will be taught by Mikey, and it will be on the value of cuteness. I know that Sheba covered some of cuteness tonight, but Mikey has a few things he wishes to add.

"We will also have Little Bit talk about brushing and other things. See you all tomorrow. It will be our last class. After that we will all need to do our share to help get the notes in order for the book."

"I don't wish to play with the notepads, at least not if Little Bit is involved," Kitten said huffily. "He'll have it all torn into pieces as soon as he gets a paw on the notes."

"Unfortunately, Kitten," Beau said seriously, "I believe you're right. Little Bit and Mikey are excused from helping with the notes."

"As elder cat in this household, I have done my share," Morris said with a wide yawn. "I'll take a look at the finished product before it goes to print to make sure you all have things in order."

"OK, Morris, you've made your point," the black cat stated firmly. "Your part in the finished product will be the final edits."

"Then it's settled. See you all tomorrow," the old cat said as he curled up to sleep.

Chapter Eleven
Brushing and Stuff

At the front of the class sat Little Bit flanked by Mikey and Sheba. "If it's all the same to everyone," Sheba announced, "Little Bit wants Mikey and me to help him with his turn tonight."

"That's fine, Sheba," Beau agreed. "Go ahead, and when you're finished, Morris and I will wrap things up. Tonight will be our last class, and it's a crucial one. Older cats need to remember the importance of brushing and cuteness beyond the obvious. Sometimes we forget a few of the basic things that help us to keep the upper paw with our humans."

"My name is Mikey, and I'm cute. My human says I am adorable. This makes me immensely happy, because it means I'll get a lot of attention and petting. Because I am cute, all of the humans play with me and give me treats. Sheba says this is because I'm a kitten, and all kittens are cute and adorable, but it won't last. She says I must remember some of the things I do that my human says are the cutest, so I can continue to do them when I grow up. Sheba is my friend. She doesn't do remarkable things to be cute, because she's a Queen. All the cats in her family are of royal blood, they don't need to be cute. She says I must learn my own ways to be cute and remember them so my human will always give me attention, treats, and lots of petting. Otherwise, my human will not remember how cute I am and be like all the others, forgetting to pet me and give me everything I want.

"I find this hard to believe, but Sheba is my friend and wouldn't lie to me, so I am going to remember the things I do and write them down so I'll remember them when I grow up.

"The older cats told me I should talk about being cute, and share it, so other cats will remember and can be cute too. One of the things I do to be cute is to roll on my back and put all four paws in the air so my human can scratch my tummy. She likes this and always gives me an immense deal of attention when I do it. It is important to have your human give you a lot of attention because when you get attention, you almost always get petting and treats."

With a poke from Sheba, Little Bit piped in "This doesn't work for digging in the plants, Mikey, even if it's fun."

"No, Little Bit, digging in the plants only makes the moms mad and no one gets any playtime. Jumping on the table to eat your mom's breakfast isn't cute either, so you shouldn't add that one on your list, Little Bit. Please remember that it always spoils the day for all of us.

"Running around the house chasing pretend mice is laudable, and so is climbing onto your human's lap to be petted. Kitten and Beau both like to play shower curtain games and jump in and out of the tub so their humans will pay attention. I don't like that though, because the one time I did it there was water in the tub, and I got all wet. Of course, the moms cuddled me in an oversized towel and made a tremendous fuss over me, but it wasn't worth getting wet. So, I recommend you look before you leap, so to speak."

"I really don't want to be here, but the older cats said it was necessary for each of us to add to this book," said Little Bit. "I'd rather write about playing jungle cat and waking up the birds because that's more fun, but the big cats say that doesn't train humans, so I'll talk about brushing. I guess I might like to be brushed if my fur weren't so long, but it tangles and is usually full of knots. That's why brushing isn't fun for me. So I guess it's important to train your human to brush you every day so your fur doesn't mat. If you're brushed every day, it doesn't hurt as much. My first humans were terribly lazy, and now my new human is trying to make up for it, but I don't like having my fur pulled or brushed the wrong way, and I try extremely hard to get away. At the same time, it isn't comfortable to have the knots in it, because they pull your skin when you move. And you have to sleep on them. I guess if she gets scratched or even gets a bite or two she'll know how much it hurts. Maybe that might make her remember to brush me more often, and that can be part of the training. It might work better than just mewing and struggling. What do you think?"

"Humans need to remember to brush short haired cats too, so they don't get so many fur-balls," Sheba added.

"Morris told me that some cats get their claws removed, which is like being mutilated, so I'm glad that hasn't happened to me. It's nicer to have a scratching post to keep my paws trimmed." Little Bit said.

"Just don't use the furniture," Mikey added. "Although it's exceptionally handy, some humans honestly don't like it when you do, even though it may help them to remember to trim your claws. If they're careful, it doesn't hurt to you get your claws trimmed, but it's sometimes fun to struggle a little anyway.

"Fleas itch, and some cats are so allergic their hair falls out when bitten. Good humans put something cold and wet on the back of our necks so we don't get fleas. Sometimes, they do it when we're in the middle of playing or sleeping, and that's inconvenient, but it's important to stay still and let them. If just one of us gets a flea, we all suffer.

"That's all we know about grooming, and we hope it helps somebody else. Though I don't know how it can help since you have to get knots or scratch up the furniture before they learn.

"Sheba told me we're not here to make humans happy. It's the other way around, so if being cute isn't fun, and it doesn't bring treats or cuddles, it isn't worth doing. Now I'm tired of this book. I'm going to play. I'm glad there won't be any more classes, because they bore me." Mikey quickly left the front of the room.

He was nearly out the door when Beau said, "Does anyone else have anything they wish to add?"

Morris yawned, jumped off the couch, and growled at Mikey to stop as he moved to the front of the room. "My great age gives me the right to retire to a life of ease and take my place as Elder Cat. I no longer consider it my duty to train our humans or teach you kittens, but I will say a few words anyway.

"In my long life, I have lived with all manner of humans—good, bad, and indifferent. But the human I have now is the best of the lot. Moreover, the others who live in our home are just as kind.

"Breakfast is on time, and fresh water is always available. The litter box is kept clean, and best of all there is always a lap ready for me to sleep on. Indeed, if my human is careless or away, there is another who will do the honor, so I need not go without or wait.

"The younger cats play and do the training when necessary to keep our humans on their toes, so I generally don't have to lift a paw. The household runs as I would like with a few exceptions, like trips to the Vet and moving. So I have little to complain about.

"Also, humans seem to live forever, but they don't. I've heard tragic tales of cats who lose their favorite human forever, and that's rough. Not only must the cat grieve the terrible loss, but also adjust to totally new circumstances at the most vulnerable time. So remember to cherish your human for everything done right, and let the human know you care.

"My advice to an elder cat is try to arrange living quarters in a home with younger cats to keep things running smoothly or find a way to live with an older human. This may not be simple, as humans who adopt a senior cat are sometimes hard to find. I guess the best thing would be to train your human well when you are both young and then grow old together. That would be ideal," Morris finished with great dignity. "Beau, I turn the floor back over to you to close our last meeting."

"Poofie has a few words he'd like to add to this book. Go ahead Poof," Beau said with a nod.

The small gray cat sat up a bit straighter. "I think we've all done a fairly admirable job training our humans. For the most part meals are served on time. We all seem to get love and cuddles when we need them, although it does seem that our humans have forgotten how to play. Or maybe it's that we who have grown a bit older would like a little different type of play, and our humans haven't yet learned the new rules, so we need to teach them. If anyone has any suggestions or new things that you have done, and think it noteworthy, please write them down and send them to us.

"We beg you not to come here for a visit, but we do appreciate the occasional letter, though it can cut into our catnaps, but we draw the line at house guests. If you've heard of new games humans play, please keep them to yourself. We have enough to keep track of," Poofie finished.

With a nod at Poof, Beau returned to his place in front of the room. "I'd like to thank you all for your patience and willingness to take part in our classes. Furthermore, Sheba, Poofie, and Champ have been working overtime to put all of our words down on paper and leave it in a place for the moms to find. We should all applaud their efforts.

"We all hope this book will help you in the training of your own human.

"Don't forget we will meet tomorrow to sort the notes," Beau yelled as the cats were all halfway out of the room.

About the Authors

Patricia Moran grew up in the Washington, DC, area. She spent most of her adult life in Northern Minnesota, where she wrote and was the photographer for the local newspaper, while she raised nine children.

In 1969 she moved to Chicago and pursued a career in community organizing, where she worked against such things as redlining. She was instrumental in getting laws against redlining implemented, while she continued to raise her four youngest children as a single mother.

She spent much of her lifetime writing or reading. She was avid at both, though much of her writing only remained in her notebooks.

Her daughter, who owns all the copyrights for her mother's work, promised her that she would finish those stories that were unfinished and publish her stories and memoir that she began in 1986.

Ms. Moran lived an extraordinary life. She lived through the Great Depression and World War II. When she was fifteen, she read to recuperating soldiers at the Red Cross who came home from the war wounded. She fell in love with a taxi driver and moved to Northern Minnesota. She was the postmistress on a Native American Reservation for a time and learned to hunt, fish, and cook.

Marta Moran Bishop lived in multiple states and countries. She is still blessed with the gift of sharing her home with multiple cats.

Ms. Bishop currently lives with her horses, cats, and a parrot named Jack on a small farm in Massachusetts.

She has multiple books, and stories in various genres, published in paperback, kindle, and recently audio.

You can find her on twitter @moranbishop, on Facebook, Google, YouTube, LinkedIn, and other social media sites. Her books are available on Amazon, Barnes and Noble, and other online stores.

www.ingramcontent.com/pod-product-compliance
Lightning Source LLC
Chambersburg PA
CBHW071826020426
42331CB00007B/1621